PUBLIC RELATIONS AND MEDIA

Mathew Knowles, M.B.A., Ph.D.

ISBN: 978-1-9995825-2-4 (Music World Publishing.

COPYRIGHT © 2018 All rights reserved world-wide under International and Pan-American copyright agreements. No part of this document can be reproduced, stored in a retrieval system, or transmitted in any form or by any means, electronic, mechanical, photocopying, recording, or otherwise without the prior written permission of Velsoft Training Materials, Inc. and Music World Publishing, Inc.

CONTENTS

Foreword v

1 Public Relations 1

2 Building Your PR Plan 7

3 Structuring Messages 15

4 Establishing Guidelines and Managing the Media 23

5 Being Interviewed 29

6 The Press Release 41

7 Providing Information to the Media 49

8 Developing Media Relationships 55

9 PR and the Crisis 61

10 Social Media and Public Relations 65

11 Speaking Under Pressure? 69

12 Focusing Your Message 79

Public Relations and New Media Work Book

1 Public Relations 95

2 Building Your PR Plan 97

3	Structuring Messages	99
4	Establishing Media Guidelines and Managing the Media	103
5	Being Interviewed	105
6	The Press Release	107
7	Providing Information to the Media	111
8	Developing Media Relationships	113
9	PR and the Crisis	115
10	Social Media and Public Relations	117

About the Author 123

FOREWORD
By Yvette Noel-Schure

Mathew Knowles is the music business executive who always knew the importance of a good press plan. We have had a great relationship over the years, but one day it almost went completely sour when Mathew complained to Donnie Ienner, the then President of Columbia Records, that I was not getting enough critical press for Destiny's Child. And by that he meant all press: urban, mainstream and international.

There were factors as to the slow down, most of it that the press was not yet ready to recognize these gorgeous, talented, young black singers from Houston, Texas, as the superstars they were born to be. But Mathew challenged me to do more and said emphatically to me that it was my job to convince them of that. And I did.

And just what was that job? It was to understand that publicity or public relations is a key factor in any success story. Whether you are promoting a music act, an event, a hospital, university, or airline, building a relationship with media networks assures accessibility to a massive audience. There are tools to the trade of course: great communication skills, an ability to be persuasive and staying on point with messaging that shapes the narrative and forces the audience to be curious about an act beyond the ten tracks on the album.

In music, it starts with a bio or biographical sketch that tells the story of an album—who wrote, arranged, and produced, but more importantly, what drives the artists. It speaks to issues that are relatable to the audience and pulls the journalist into saying yes to knowing more. And for Mathew Knowles, it was important that those stories were written globally, from the US, Europe, Africa, South America, Australia, and Asia.

It is that exchange between the media and the talent, in many cases, that shapes the audience's decision to believe in the act and then to invest in the act with album sales, streaming, and to purchase concert tickets to shows around the world.

Mathew Knowles has always known that press was a key ingredient in any marketing plan. He understood early the avenue that goes from the journalist to the audience that in turn benefits the act. In this digital media age, a lot has change in the publicity space but some things remain the same. People listen to the voices of influential people and we all tune in to one form of media, whether TV, digital, or radio for our information.

In these pages, Mathew Knowles delves into everything, from the importance of the interview to controlling the narrative and structuring the messages. It comes from a proven executive who started from the ground up, learned the business, formed relationship in every sector, and who wasn't and isn't afraid of the next challenge.

About Yvette Noel-Schure

Yvette Noel-Schure has developed press campaigns for a diverse roster of artists, including Mariah Carey, Will Smith, Jessica Simpson, Prince, John Legend, Adele, Wyclef Jean, Maxwell, Destiny's Child and each of the group's members: Kelly Rowland, Michelle Williams, and Beyoncé.

1
PUBLIC RELATIONS

The field of public relations and new media has changed and continues to evolve with changes in technology, the ease with which people and news can travel, and how journalists and the public interact.

Introduction

The field of public relations has changed dramatically due to the presence and evolution of the Internet. It used to be that the company could issue a press release, arrange for a press conference, and speak directly to journalists who would pass their message along. In turn, the public would receive these releases by reading them in a newspaper, watching the television news, or listening to the radio.

That's no longer the case. Changes in the way we seek and receive our information mean that the company can virtually think a thought, and have it released to the media within minutes, whether they wanted it to be that way or not.

The proliferation of social media and common use of tools such as cellphones mean that messages can be released from a company and "go viral" almost instantly. One of the challenges for public relations is that the goal is to create a very well-crafted message before it gets out among the public, but to do that can be very difficult.

Not that long ago, when newspapers gave us most of the news we needed, the paper could print a story and then later print a retraction. These days, things are very different. News gets carried by social media at a rapid pace, and in so many directions, that a retraction may go nowhere at all, while the original—albeit erroneous—story goes as far as it can.

If someone within the company learns something new, they can literally share it with all their friends in mere moments. As a result, it becomes even more important that we spread news that is worthy of being shared and sends the message that we intended.

Naturally, many companies do a good job with their public relations. They have dedicated communicators on staff who understand their own jobs and who create a message that reflects the organization's brand and mission. They will also carefully craft a message that can be effectively and efficiently released through social media and be picked up virally while spreading the image of the company that they want to share.

What Public Relations Is All About

Public relations, often referred to as PR, is the methodology that companies use to help spread their messages, usually through advertising and marketing efforts. It is also a term we use to refer to the communications strategy that a company uses. With the increased acceptance and reliance on the internet, PR is positioned to work with every department in an organization, assisting the leadership in managing their messages.

A person who works in PR can be referred to by different terms, including PR Specialist, PR Consultant, Communications Consultant, and PR Manager. There are three major influences that are contributing to a raised profile for PR consultants: fragmentation, saturation, and reputation.

Fragmentation

When people got most of their news from a newspaper or television, it was a straightforward exercise to find your audience. To get their attention, a smartly designed advertising campaign could capture your target's attention and perhaps even gain you some press coverage.

Nowadays, more people than ever actually get their news and entertainment through the internet, and there are so many "channels" available that it can be very difficult to find, and capture the attention of, your target audience. There are people who do not listen to local radio, watch local TV news, or read newspapers at all, because they prefer to get their information from other sources.

Saturation

As consumers, we are inundated with messages to such a level that we tune them out because there is just no way to absorb the number of ads to which we are exposed. This makes the PR job even more difficult because you must find a way to stand out and establish your products or services effectively.

Reputation

Your company is open to more scrutiny than ever, as the Internet provides an easy way for your customers—and adversaries—to talk about you via short messages, blogs, live discussions, and forums. And they really do talk, so it's essential that you are aware of, and able to mitigate, any damage if things go awry.

You may have already figured out that traditional advertising is no longer the best (or only) way for you to distribute your messages. As fragmentation, saturation, and reputation become more prevalent, they also point us toward the need to strategic application of PR in order to get our message past, and in front of, the competition.

What it Means to Get Strategic

If old-style PR included advertising in print, television, and radio media, and revealed a 'life of' to share daily experiences with their fans. However, those methods are no long as pertinent as they were, how do we get heard? We must be strategic and think about the bigger picture, instead of being tactical and following an outdated process.

For example, as I wrote this course I was delighted to watch two colleagues launch their new album. At one time, they would have had a album launch party in a local record store, they may have asked a couple of prominent people to write album reviews to appear in the paper prior to the release of the album, and their publisher would have provided them with a marketing campaign budget.

Instead, the Artists created a PR strategy around the album. They developed a website with a URL that is the same as the title of the album, talked about how great their publisher was (even though there had been no advance or marketing budget provided), spoke anywhere they could, attended trade shows, and held writing classes for other aspiring Artists.

They developed a social media strategy that included having everyone they knew participating in sharing and forwarding messages. Their blogs, and the blogging that other people were doing, also helped to promote the album. They also volunteered to appear on the local breakfast television newscast. One bonus of that breakfast television spot was that in the hour leading up to their "spot," the news anchor and program hosts mentioned the title of the album and a little blurb at least four times!

The cost of this publicity program was far less than taking out a full-page ad in the newspaper (which in medium to large markets can be up to $50,000 for ad design and advertising fees), and they certainly got people talking about the album. On its first day, the album reached the Billboard chart's list, and it sold out by day two.

Notes

2
BUILDING YOUR PR PLAN

Everyone needs a plan! It doesn't need to be written in stone; in fact, it needs to be flexible so that you can make changes that reflect your working environment. However, a plan provides a roadmap to follow as well to achieve our goals.

Defining Reality

Plan, plan, plan, and then the execution is easy, right? We're used to project planning principles in a lot of our work, and public relations is no exception. It takes skill to create eloquent press releases and to reach your target market, but it takes greater skill and strategy to get the results that you are looking for. Before you get started, you'll need to get a very good understanding of what's happening within your organization, your industry, and among the competition.

You've also got to do something important to create a good public relations strategy. You've got to create a strong foundation, in the same way that the foundation is what supports a new house. You need to ask yourself the following questions, in order, and before you dive in and implement your PR plan!

- How do we make money (where does our revenue come from)?
- Who are the customers who generate most of our revenue?
- Who is our target customer and what is it they want from us?
- Who among our stakeholders are making decisions about our products or services?
- Who is our competition, and what are they up to in terms of positioning and promotions?
- How do we currently differentiate ourselves from the competition?
- How is the marketplace changing toward our products or services (growing, shrinking, maintaining)?
- What are our business objectives for the next three, six, nine, and twelve months? What is our plan beyond that?
- What are the results of our analysis of strengths, weaknesses, opportunities, and threats?
- What are the pertinent details of our current business, strategic, and marketing plans in place?
- Are we prepared (and in what ways) for any kind of crisis intervention?
- What are the implications for PR communications as we look forward?

- What is our plan or product story?
- Who are the influencers?

Overall, your PR plan will include the following phases:

- Defining story
- Defining the goal
- Choosing your strategy and tactics
- Implementing your plan
- Evaluating and reviewing the plan

Defining the Story

In today's market place, the consumer buys the story first; the product second. No different from if a sales rep was selling a product to a customer. First the decision maker buys the sales rep first, and then their product. The same concept made me a success with 12 years as a sale rep in the medical diagnostic field. It's even critical today now that we have so many types of platforms that consumers can go to.

How did we come about the product? What differentiates our product from others? How did we come up with product? It can be a person place or thing, either way, folks want to hear the success and struggle in putting out products and the story becomes a critical part. Focus on a prepared story to present any product. Your narrative is paramount! Very important!

Defining the Goal

Once you have completed your research and defined reality from the previous section, you are ready to look at your goals. Keeping two or three clear goals in mind means that you can create a campaign that can get you the results you need, because you are directing your efforts at what is required.

Each time you undertake a PR campaign, you need to be very clear on the goals you are striving for. Be clear on the fact that advertising and PR are not the same thing. Advertising is the way your company promotes a product, offers a deal, and tries to get the attention of consumers. PR goes further than that, using strategies that are built on solid communication skills to engage more customers and employees in the mission and vision of the organization.

Where advertising can be used to describe features and benefits of your products or services, PR can offer client testimonials and add an authoritative appeal to spreading the news of that same product. (People will not believe what a company says about their product anywhere near as quickly as they will tolerate the onslaught of messages that come from satisfied customers and actual users.)

PR can provide several functions, including:

- Strengthening your brand awareness
- Increasing the demand for your products or services
- Generating trust with customers.
- Shifting public perceptions about what you make/sell
- Helping position your company and/or product as a leader in the marketplace

You need to decide beforehand to which function(s) your campaign will appeal. In doing so, you're going to connect with the stakeholders in your company, which is good, because you also need their support and full buy-in to the program if you are going to get what you need out of it.

One mistake that newly minted PR specialists make is that they want to push their own agenda forward. They are confident that they know what the company needs and how to get it, and they think that their way is the only way to get something done. But you must temper that knowledge and enthusiasm and direct it appropriately. You may know all of these things but pushing your agenda may just raise the ire of the very people you need support from. Instead, set your agenda aside.

Ask your stakeholders what they expect, what needs are unmet from previous campaigns, and what they see as priorities. This will help you to establish a trusting relationship with stakeholders, especially when they realize that you really have set your personal agenda aside, and you are listening to their needs.

People you may need to approach for this level of support may include:

- CEO
- Executive team
- Board of directors
- Internal PR/communications team, and any external providers involved
- Sales and marketing team(s)

And don't forget your front-line ambassadors: every single employee!

Selecting Your Strategy and Tactics

We know that using tactics will get us a certain distance, but that PR programs become more successful with higher results and better market penetration when they are built on strategy.

Strategy includes plans for:

- Attracting stakeholder support

- Building your PR team (internal or external)
- Understanding your target customer/audience
- Leveraging trends/technology
- Have a compelling message
- Build relationships
- Use feedback wisely
- Measure and monetize results
- Developing a relevant program

Tactics are the specifics of how you will get your messages heard:

- Inviting stakeholders to a meeting
- Hiring staff or contracting a PR firm
- Meeting customers at an event
- Writing a press release, article, or blog post
- Calling a reporter to give them news about your company
- Posting messages and looking for traffic on social media platforms

The Plan

Whether you are building a PR plan for a small product launch or looking at your next 12 months, you've got to create a plan that you can follow. Using the information that you've already learned, we're confident that you can create a strategy for your public relations program, and so the next step is to create a plan for something specific.

These are the steps you will follow:

- Outline the reality
- Define the goals
- Describe your strategy
- Set up a tactics list
- Define benchmarks
- Implement the plan
- Work in some flexibility
- Evaluate, review, and repeat

Next, we'll discuss each step.

Outline the Reality

Be very clear on what your situation is, who you support/stakeholders are, what your budget is, what the limitations are. This is aided if you complete a SWOT (strengths, weaknesses, opportunities, threats) analysis, although you do not do one general SWOT analysis for each PR plan you launch as you may have typically experimented with in the past: you must do one for each aspect of your plan.

Define the Goals for This Plan

What are you trying to achieve? Are you building a broader reach for a particular product or service? Is your priority in improving the company image? How about attracting staff who can align with the company values and will stick around for a while?

Describe Your Strategy

You should be able to speak about your strategy to stakeholders in a way that they immediately know what it is, how they are involved, and what the outcomes are.

Set Up a Tactics List

This is the list of how you will reach your goals. You can include things like press releases, articles, interviews, press conferences, and much more here.

Define Benchmarks

This is your to-do list, and the order that you will set up your communications. It should be something that other members of your team can refer to keep themselves on track and includes the dates and measurements that you will utilize. In your absence or in case of a crisis, your team will refer to this list to help mitigate any damages, so it's essential that you keep it up to date.

Implement the Plan

Do what you have said you will do, on time, and within budget. This helps you reach your goals (celebrate!) and builds trust within your organization and with your customer base that you do what you say you will do.

Work in Some Flexibility

There are things that we cannot predict that will surface. Your competition could beat you to market with a similar product to the one you are about release; you could be faced with a recall of your product; workers can go on strike anywhere along the production or distribution chain;

transportation or distribution can fail. Create a contingency plan so that you are available and capable to handle anything unexpected.

Notes

STRUCTURING MESSAGES

Communication skills can be learned. If you don't feel you are the best person to convey public messages, you can learn to do so at a much higher level.

When you live your passion, you never work a day in your life.
—Mathew Knowles, M.B.A., Ph.D.
The DNA of Achievers: 10 Traits of Highly Successful Professionals

Creating Your Media Image

When people think of a media image, they think about wearing the right clothes and saying the right things. These are important, but only part of what contributes to your media image.

Managing your image is about how you present yourself and your company, and about being congruent in the way you do so. The way that you present your company to the public must be carefully managed.

Getting Clear on Your Message

What are the mission, vision, and values of your company? What is your strategic plan? Does the way you talk, dress, and present yourself in public make you a good representation of what you stand for? If so, great! If not, why not? What are you willing to do to make yourself congruent with what you say you stand for?

Developing a Media Package

A well-done media package can contain a lot of useful information that answers a journalist's question before they even know they have it.

A media package can be a very powerful and helpful tool if done right. It is your chance to provide all the relevant information you think a member of the media will need regarding your company or a person.

Think about fishing, a media package is like the bait on your hook, it draws the media in. Media packages are handed out a press conferences and sometimes included with press releases for a complete presentation.

Bios

When your media package is designed to promote or introduce an individual you must include a bio. A comprehensive bio should include enough personal information to flesh out the person's character. In most cases, it should lean heavily on the person's professional life and accomplishments as it is likely a tool for promoting a person in a professional aspect.

Think about the basics, what a journalist is going to ask right up front and provide that information in the bio. Include a quote or two from the person as well. It will either spur a journalist to contact you to expand into a story or a lazy one (yes, they do exist!) will just copy and paste and call it a day. Therefore, in that case, you will be glad that you presented the best possible media bio that you could.

Company History

For those times when your media package is all about putting a company in the spotlight you've got to give the media the goods. You've got to include company history, and this includes significant figures, accomplishments, people, and products.

You don't have to go overboard with details but give the media enough information on the company itself, that includes where it's been and where it's going, so that they can develop a story that is well-rounded.

Headshots, Logos, Graphics, Stats, Video/Audio Clips

This section deals with the nuts and bolts of a media package. A good media package contains many elements but there are certain components that must be included in every one of them.

- You need headshots of the main person, or people, mentioned in the package.
- If the media package is dealing with a company rather than a specific person, you should include copies of any corporate logos or graphics. These should be included in both electronic and hard copy forms.
- You might want to include files (hard copy, or electronic) of any stats you want noted.
- Include links and addresses for relevant online resources too.

Depending on what type of media you aim to target with your media package, it would be a good idea to include audio and video files. They can add a whole other dimension to your package.

Contact Details

Of course, all the above is moot, if it's difficult, or impossible for members of the media to reach you after you've released a media package for yourself or your company.

Put all your contact information on the package and when you can be reached if you will be out of touch at some point. Include your contact information in more than one place in the package as well, just to be sure. Adding a physical business card never hurts as well.

A media package can include a variety of items, including:

- Photos and captions of company leaders, community involvement, or other positive messages, which must also include copyright/attribution information
- Q & A (Question and Answers) about the company

- Previous news releases
- Copies of articles previously published
- Biographies and backgrounds about key stakeholders
- Photos of executives or products
- Product or service listing
- Achievements/awards received
- Albums, movies, or films
- Annual reports, brochures, or publications
- CD, DVD or MP3 files with previous media coverage, or video clips of company headquarters that a media outlet can use to complement a story

For an award ceremony, your media package might include some of the following:

- Background to the awards.
- List of sponsors.
- Biographies of the award winners.
- Samples of the products or ideas that led to the award.

This might include photos, artwork, posters, or whatever else you can think of!

During a crisis, the media package should also include reports, photo or video samples, police or investigative reports, witness statements, court or safety investigation documents, and whatever else relates to the event.

Here is an example of a media package that would apply to a company when they are redesigning their logo:

- A press release with a catchy title, like: "Coffee Company Claims Cup"
- A tip sheet for attendees to make the most of an upcoming party celebrating the new design
- A "History of the Cup" that provides full color, glossy posters placed throughout the room and highlighting the 50-year history of this great company
- A well written corporate "backgrounder" on the company owners, from inception to today
- Biographies of the current owners and top executive
- Photo quality copies of the new logo

Attention to Style

Items in the media package need to look like they are all part of the same brand to give them a professional look. In addition, when you are sending information to a news service, it needs to look like it was written for a journalist. To do that well, most people use The Associated Press Style Book and Briefing on Media Law as a standard resource, but it is always a good idea for you to see what the standards are in your region.

Creating Strong, Positive Messages

Before you start creating messages with a goal of getting them to the media, we have some guidelines for you to consider. Our goal is to help you create messages that catch the attention of the media as well as your customers. People are bombarded with advertising and media messages now that everyone is on electronic device (such as tablets, smartphones, and computers).

They may even be watching television in the background! You must craft a message that gets heard through the fray.

Your messages should follow the MEDIA model.

Make it Positive

Always release messages that are positive. You can put a positive light on anything, even a disaster, and positive messages put your organization in the best light. You also need to make sure that anyone who is involved in delivering messages to the public (including the people standing near you in a public meeting or press announcement) have confident postures, don't roll their eyes, and they know how to speak clearly and positively as well.

Elaborate on the 5 W's

Your messages need to be complete. Refer to what you learned about writing in school, and leverage the who, what, where, when, why (and how) so that you do not miss any important details.

Draw an Image

People may not remember what you say, unless you do it in a way that touches them on a level that is beyond the words that you speak or write. Create messages that connect to their emotions and engage them in creating a picture in their mind, so that they are more likely to remember at least the important aspects of your message.

Influence

Your message must have a purpose, and often that will be to exert influence or persuade someone to take action once they have internalized the message. You may want them to try out your product or say something positive about your latest invention. Whatever it is, your own talent can be honed by studying powerful messages from negotiators, mediators, and sales professionals.

Announce

So, you've been busy for months working in secret on the newest, greatest product your company has ever developed, when WHAM!

A disgruntled employee releases the news far before you are ready.

In that kind of case, you need to make an announcement to the public and mitigate any damage or rumors circulating. The best thing you can do as a PR specialist is to craft your messages, set up press releases, or respond to a crisis as soon as possible so that you control the timing, impact, and format of any announcement.

Social media adds a whole new twist to public relations. Instant information means you have less control over what the public has access to, and it makes your role much more important.

—Mathew Knowles, M.B.A., Ph.D.

Notes

ESTABLISHING GUIDELINES AND MANAGING THE MEDIA

Standard operating procedures help you know what to do and when. While some people are opposed to structure or formality in their work, the benefits outweigh the work or frustration, as people get clear on what they should and should not do.

Defining Guidelines

Depending on the size of your company, you might be the only person answering the phone and thereby responsible for any media or public inquiries. Or perhaps a journalist calls you but must go through someone else first. Either way, everyone in your organization needs to know how to best respond to those inquiries, who to direct a call or foot traffic to, and how they should reply to a persistent individual.

Media guidelines can take care of all of that. They explain your company's approach to relationship building with the media, how information will be shared, and how much.

Your media guidelines could include things like:

- All media inquiries and inquiries from people you consider could be media (bloggers, citizen journalists, etc.) must be directed to the Communications Officer.
- Media inquiries must get a response within six hours.

There are plenty of options when it comes to media guidelines. It all depends on what your goals are and what your public relations plan looks like.

Selecting a Spokesperson

In a small company, it's probably the CEO who will do most announcements and have most interactions with the media. As the company gets larger, a CFO (Chief Financial Officer) may be the person who speaks to financial matters, while the CIO (Chief Information Officer) speaks to great technological work the company does. In a crisis, there may be a Communications Officer who becomes the liaison between the company and the media, allowing the CEO time and space to focus on the actual crisis. In a large company, there may be several spokespeople who can each speak about their areas of expertise.

There are some essential elements to consider in determining who the spokesperson will be.

Select Great Communicators

If you are the CEO and you know you are not a great communicator, then you need to sharpen those skills. Your credibility is increased when you speak well, when you can listen to questions and answer thoughtfully, and when people believe what you say. These skills can all be learned. In fact, most of us can improve our communication skills.

Find Ambassadors

Your spokespeople need to be positive supports for the company. They need passion as well as expertise and they need to be able to communicate that to their audience. Their body language, facial expressions, and overall attitude need to support the message, and it also helps if they can build relationships with members of the media rather than simply make statements. Relationships will lead to more thorough understanding by members of the media. It can't hurt to make a few friends!

Interpersonal Counts

Some people are not great spokespeople, no matter how fantastic they are technically. If you have people on your team who are not cut out to withstand the media frenzy, cannot think on the spot, or are not easily likeable, have someone else deliver their message. In the spokesperson role, it's vitally important to find people who are easy to get along with, outgoing, and can develop relationships easily, not technical experts.

Strong Insight is Important

A spokesperson needs to hear what's behind a reporter's question, and to try to understand the intent behind it.

Approval Process

As part of your creation of guidelines, you also must create (or be a part of) an approval process. A series of approvals is often necessary before a news release, marketing campaign, or annual report, for example, are released to the media and the public. This helps stop any errors of fact or release of information prematurely, and to prepare for any questions that come because of that information.

There are often several rounds of approval required, so it's a good idea for you to develop patience and not be too invested in the copy that you write. You will fret, re-work, and redesign a release only to have it go through several layers of approval and come back to you looking quite different. Let go of any personal attachment you must the work and focus on the process of creating information that works for the people you work with, and that is useful, accurate, purposed information for the media and public.

Managing the Media

Manage your business, or your business manages you, right? You'll need to take the same approach with media: developing relationships, growing community, and being responsible all support your business' success.

Building Rapport with Reporters

Reporters are your ally and offer you access to the media, and so you want to work well with them. There are several things that you can do to both engage reporters and to make sure that they are able to get your information into circulation.

Be Approachable

Gone are the days when a journalist had 72 hours to pull together a story. We live in an instantaneous news environment and if they call you for a quote for a story that is being published in 30 minutes, they will simply report that you were "unavailable to answer our call." Instead, and especially if there is something going on that puts your company in the news, make yourself available.

Create Stellar Media Package

Give journalists the information they need to understand issues before they even ask for it.

Be Newsworthy

Invite reporters into your place of business when you have something interesting and notable to share with them. Don't waste their time with the usual. Try to look at things from their point of view: what captures news interest in your region, who and what are the compelling topics and generate the most response to a particular news story?

Be Professionally Distant yet Likeable

If you have one journalist that you rely on give them exclusive access, that can help build your image. However, you can also be perceived as stand offish or unavailable to all the other media sources out there. Think long and hard about how you want to be perceived. We don't recommend that you become best friends with one journalist; instead, aim for some professional distance and develop relationships with lots of journalists.

Become a Good Speaker

If you are not used to speaking with reporters, you need to practice. Consider joining an organization like Toastmasters and hone your speaking skills to a professional level.

Notes

BEING INTERVIEWED

If you've never been interviewed by the media before, it can be a nerve wracking experience. Even if you're a season spokesperson there are always things to remember and things not to answer.

As a Citizen

Saying No to an Interview Request

When you get contacted by a member of the media, remember that there's no obligation upon you to be interviewed. That is unless you're an elected official or press contact for your organization. You don't have to answer any questions, it's not like you're being questioned on the witness stand.

It seems that some people think if they get contacted by a journalist, that they must answer. It's not true. Just say no. It's that easy. If you have nothing important to say, or more to add, or have no knowledge of the topic, then just say so and pass on the interview. If you wish to agree to the interview, but need more time, then tell the interviewer. Ask for more time and agree upon a time for an interview, or for the release of a prepared statement.

Being contacted by a member of the media, especially out of the blue, can be upsetting or surprising. If you are put in this situation, remember that the journalist contacted you and you are not powerless in this situation. Don't just agree on reflex to answer any questions.

Remain Calm

If you do agree to an interview request the first thing to remember is to remain calm. Whether it's a radio interview, a print interview or a spot on TMZ, don't get flustered with thoughts of your words being granted permanence in some archival state somewhere.

Being interviewed, if you're not used to it, or unprepared, can be nerve wracking. But remember, as the subject being interviewed that you have quite a bit of control, you can control the pace of the interview.

- You can ask for questions to be repeated or explained further.
- Don't rush with your answers.
- Be concise, don't ramble. Answers shouldn't be more than 30 seconds initially. If the reporter wants more, they'll ask more questions.
- Provide facts and examples.
- When you're done talking, stop talking. Don't be uncomfortable with silence, it's an old journalism tool to get people to say more to fill in the 'dead air'.

- If you're the type of person who tends to speak quickly when nervous, keep telling yourself to slow down.

- Keep your cool, don't be goaded into saying something you will regret. As the one answering the questions, you dictate the message you are delivering, or the comments you want to make.

If you're answering an email interview, make sure you read your answers closely and edit them. If possible, get someone else to read them to before hitting the send button. If it's someone who is familiar with the topic of the interview, that's even better.

Listen to the Question

Listening is an underrated skill that can't be overstated when you are dealing with the media.

When being interviewed, or asked for comment on some issue, that request is going to likely come in the form of a question. That sounds simple enough, but the real trick is to listen to what is being said. Don't assume you know what the questioner is going to ask. Take your time, listen to the question, then take some more time and formulate your response. As we mentioned earlier, you are in control when you are the one being asked a question.

If you don't understand the question or are unsure what the questioner wants to know—just ask. Don't assume you know what they are asking. Rephrase the question and repeat it back to them if you must for your own clarity.

Of course, this is somewhat easier with a written question, such as an email. You can read it multiple times and get advice on the question if you're unsure.

Once you're sure you know what the questioner wants to know then you must come up with an answer. This is where you get the chance to state your case or pass along your message.

- If you don't understand the question or are unsure what the questioner wants to know—just ask.

- Don't assume you know what they are asking.

- Rephrase the question and state it back to them if you must.

- Always take a few seconds, three seconds is the recommended time for an interview, before answering. It helps you marshal your thoughts and give an answer you are happy with.

- If you think the reporter may not have understood your answer don't be afraid to repeat it. You can also ask the reporter if they understood what you were trying to say.

Be Honest

Honesty truly is the best policy. It doesn't pay to lie or dance around the truth. You're better off saying outright "I'm not going to answer that question" than to lie. Currently, it's very easy to be found out if you're untruthful. That can be very damaging to you, your career, or your organization. Your reputation is one of the most precious commodities you have. Protect it.

Slander/Libel

In the world of keyboard warriors who hide behind the anonymity of the Internet when posting hurtful or spiteful comments, discourse can sink to the level of libel very quickly. (A very rough definition of the types of defamation is that slander is spoken, and libel is written.)

When speaking with the media, what you say must be defendable, otherwise you are running the risk of legal sanctions. There are certain defenses that you can use to defend yourself against charges of defamation.

Some of these defenses are: truth, privilege, opinion, fair comment, and lack of damages. Providing any kind of legal advice, or a concise legal definition, is beyond the scope of this book. If necessary, consult professional legal help in your area.

Being honest is one way to guarantee accuracy in your comments to the media. Lies are hard to remember—stick to the truth.

Interview Preparation

If you know ahead of time that you are going to be dealing with the media, then that's to your advantage as you have time to prepare and practice what you are going to say.

Think ahead of time about questions that you may be asked and have answers prepared for them. Think about issues that you are involved in or would be asked to comment upon. If you have the chance, ask the journalist ahead of time what the interview is going to be about.

Familiarize yourself with your prepared answers so you can deliver them smoothly. It's also a good chance to see if there's any mistakes in your answers, or if there's anything you would like to expand upon or add. Familiarize yourself especially with the person interviewing you understand their strengths and weaknesses.

It doesn't hurt to practice answering questions from another person, get a colleague or friend to ask you the type of questions you expect. Maybe get them to throw an unexpected one or two in their as well, just to keep you sharp. Thinking on your feet is a skill that's very valuable, and preparation can help with that as well.

If you've got the time and the resources, film, or at least record the audio of your practice interview, that way you can debrief yourself and make any changes you feel you require.

As a Media Spokesperson

As a spokesperson, it is your professional duty to be available to the media to respond to their requests for interviews or statements. It's also part of your job to secure the proper spokesperson for a certain topic if that is more appropriate. For example, suppose you as a media contact for an aircraft manufacturer who has just released a fully electric airliner. You may be able to speak generally about the project, but it would likely be better to have one of the engineers available for the media.

Some of the same principles for dealing with the media apply to the average citizen and media spokesperson alike. Two of the main ones are listen and be honest.

Stick to the message, message length, key points.

As a media spokesperson, you have a job to do, and that job is it to get across your organization's message. Even if you are the one being contact by the media, and not the initiator, it's up to you to remain on message, make your point know as best you can.

Clarify with your organization and your supervisors beforehand what message to deliver. Practice it and have a copy of your statement ready for the media. Keep the message a reasonable length when responding to the media. Don't ramble, but also don't be so short that you don't get your message out there.

You will have key points to make as a media spokesperson, they are part of the message. Hitting all your points reinforces your message.

If you say you'll get back to them, get back to them

Some members of the media are slave to deadlines for part of their work, think TV, radio, and newspaper reporters. They all have deadlines to meet for broadcast or press times. (They also have online components that they can fill, but usually there aren't the strictures of deadlines associated with them.)

So, to a member of the media that must meet a deadline, the best thing you can be is available and prompt. If you are unavailable at the time they try to contact you, but your voicemail says you will return their call as soon as possible, do it, don't put them off. Even if all you have to say is that you need more time, then let them know. It's a sign of professionalism and respect.

These are two factors that are important when developing a relationship with members of the media, which is a topic we will cover later.

No Comment

If you don't have the answer to a question, just say so. Don't hide behind 'no comment'. Think about how many times you have seen someone being interviewed on TV and they say that. Think about how they look, like either they don't know what they're doing, they're lying, or they're hiding something.

It may be uncomfortable for you, but simply say 'I don't have an answer for you now about that. But I will get back to you.' If the media member continues to press, say that you don't have all the information needed to answer the question properly and will take the time to get what you need so that you can do your job effectively.

But, and this gets back to deadlines, if you say you are going to get back the media person with more information, do that, don't run and hide, it's not your job as a media spokesperson to be unavailable or unreliable.

Dig up More Information if Needed

For those times when you are temporarily stumped by a question, make note of what the question is, what information you need to answer it, and where you can get that information.

Follow up on those points and get the information you need. Then consider the question further and think of any follow-up questions that could arise from that information and then pursue it so that you are fully prepared should those follow-ups arise.

Find the Correct Source

There may be times when you aren't comfortable, capable, or qualified to respond to a media question. For example, you are a spokesperson for a university and one of the professors in the medical school has come up with a major neurosurgery breakthrough. Unless you are a neurosurgeon yourself, it would make perfect sense to direct any media inquiries to that specific professor.

Be Available for Follow Up

It's part and parcel of a media spokesperson's job to be available to the media, even after hours. Different media outlets work on different schedules, online news is 24/7 so sometimes you are going to get contacted outside traditional working hours. Do your best to be available to members of the media, it will go a long way to establishing a productive working relationship with them.

Communications Officer

A communications officer can be viewed differently than a spokesperson is some cases. We are going to consider the communications officer that works more behind the scenes, rather than out front like a spokesperson in this instance.

Keep Communications Person in the Loop

Communications officers are responsible for writing press releases, press statements, speeches, open letters, and other forms of communication, just as the job title says. But, they must know what's going on in the company or organization to be able to do their job successfully.

So, if you are dealing with the media as part of your job, and your company also has a communications officer, make sure you keep them in the loop. It's important for the communications officer to know what you've said in a press statement, for example, in case they are called upon to follow up on that statement, with a clarification or more information.

They can't do their job in a vacuum, so when you're dealing with the media, keep the communications person in the back of your mind too. This will really pay off if you need some quick assistance or research done, if the communications officer is up to speed, they can be of much more help than if they are in the dark.

You should include your communications officer on your contact list to CC any media emails to them as well.

Answering Tough Questions

Whether you are faced with an exciting new product release, a new artists album or an announcement about a charity fundraiser you are involved in, or you are managing a crisis, someone is going to ask you some hard questions. They can come at you at any time.

You've probably seen examples of this when a company spokesperson is announcing one thing, and a reporter starts asking questions about a different topic, and practically derails the session.

When it comes to answering tough questions, we have some tips for you that will help you stay calm, and to answer the questions professionally and easily. Since these types of questions are much easier to answer in isolation (as in this course), we strongly recommend that you practice the technique several times before you get into the public eye.

When asked a tough question, here is your strategy:

Pause

Resist the temptation to jump right in and say something because you can never ever take it back. Take a few moments to make sure you understand the question and collect your thoughts on the matter.

Restate the Question

If you think there could be a misunderstanding, or you need a little bit more time, restate the question and then ask if you have it right.

You can restate it word for word, or take a wordy question and make it shorter: "Joel, if I understand your question, you are asking…"

Return the Question

Sometimes a question is inappropriate for the time. While avoiding it may hamper your relationship with the journalist who asks, sometimes this need to be managed this way to stop a press conference or news interview from getting off track. You can politely say, "Joel, that question is not part of what we are discussing here today. Why don't we meet in an hour, and I can discuss it with you then?" You can also say, "What would you do if you were in my position," which might deflect the spotlight from you long enough to collect your thoughts.

Resist the Urge to Fake It

If you are asked a question about something to which you lack information, be honest and admit that you need more information to answer that question, and then demonstrate your high level of integrity by following up with an answer when you have the information.

Answer the Question Honestly

People appreciate when you show your human side and do not try to hide behind the corporation. If you make a mistake, admit it. If you do something stupid, admit it and add an apology as well as reparation if possible.

Don't Ever, Ever Lie

You will damage your credibility and may never get it back.

Use a Coach

If you are going to be in the media a lot (like politicians, sports coaches, athletes, and big companies with environmental or people issues, for example), get yourself a coach. A coach can help you prepare for and field tough questions, making them much easier.

Observe Others

Watch interviews and learn from them. See what politicians, CEOs, and regular people do to manage all questions, from the easy to the tough.

Practice, Practice, Practice

There is no substitution or shortcut for it.

Speaking in Sound Bites

If you start thinking about news reports, whether on television or a YouTube video, you'll probably have come across the sound bite. A sound bite is an easily shared, highly quotable piece of information that can be run repeatedly before the news story itself airs.

This might be your press release conveyed through a clearly spoken 20 seconds, or an idea, or a newsworthy tantalizing element of a project. Journalists love sound bites, because they need all those areas of otherwise dead time filled during their news program. If you can wrap up what you do in a sound bite, you'll endear yourself to journalists everywhere.

While you are preparing for a news conference, writing a news release or planning for your company web release (your own YouTube video, for example), try to incorporate a real sound bite. A sound bite can be what makes you stand out among your competition because you've said something that breaks through the noise pollution and caught their attention!

Your sound bite needs to follow the SIM model:

- Short
- Intriguing
- Memorable

You must be able to deliver your sound bite in 15 seconds if the media is going to be able to use it. That's 15 quick seconds, and not 18 or 20. You'll use your sound bite to catch people's attention. Think of it like the sales person's elevator pitch, or your verbal business card. The beauty of a sound bite is that if forces you to get really clear on your message.

Start with a message that is 30 seconds or less, that you really can deliver in an elevator or at a networking meeting.

Then get it down to 15 seconds so that you can fit it into any kind of media profile. It needs to include:

- Who you are (or you company)
- What you do (try to position it in a way that helps you stand out from your competition)
- How you do it differently than anyone else

Here Are Some Examples:

- I'm Joel Mitcham from MoneyServe, where I free people from financial stresses. I can do the same for you. We're celebrating the launch of our freedom savers program where you can make more money in less time and support local charities.
- I am an image consultant and coach and I teach people to work on being rich from the inside out, because once the inside is in alignment the outside follows suit.
- I used to weigh an extra hundred pounds, and I have kept it off for four years. I can help you get your body into the shape you want it to be without working as hard as I had to.
- We're launching a program to help people get control of their mess at home or in the business place with absolutely zero stress.
- We're an oil exploration company who has just put finishing touches on a camp for kids with a gift for science and math.
- I'm Louise Marchello from Insights Incorporated, and we find places for people to live no matter what stage of their life they are at: first place, bigger space, downsizing, grandkids moving in, or retirement living. We do it all over the country!
- I'm Tanya and my new album offers the best in pop and R&B. My approach is that each song will have its own video. Which is for you to see the music as well as hearing the music.

Options When You Have "No Comment"

There will be times when you are not ready or able to provide the media with information. This can happen when you are waiting for the leadership team to work through a crisis and come up with an action plan, when you are required to react to rumors but not yet ready, or when the media gets wind of something you are unprepared to talk about.

You may have seen politicians, sports figures, and actors try to say, "no comment" to a journalist. Sometimes a journalist will respect the "no comment" comment, and other times they will push for something more.

When you are compelled to say, "no comment" and are being ignored, we have some suggestions for getting yourself the time you need to research, react, and reply.

Be Honest

If you do not have the information that you need, don't try to bluff your way past the press. It only strains the relationship between you and the media. That relationship needs to be built on trust, and that comes from being truthful.

Be Thoughtful

In a crisis especially, emotions run high. Resist the urge to be angry, defensive, or to vent. This is not the time to say, "I'd like my life back," which BP's Tony Hayward did following the BP disaster in the Gulf of Mexico in 2010. Think before you speak.

Ask

Instead of pushing a reporter away, simply ask them for help as you collect the information that you need. If you get a call about an incident you have not even heard of yet, and if you've developed a good working relationship with your media contact, they will cut you some slack and give you some time if they have it available. Keep in mind though, that time frames are short and you won't have much time as you gather your information and your thoughts, and craft your response.

The phrase "no comment" is not a phrase you should ever utter to the media, because you will leave them with no options except to find answers elsewhere. If you are the public relations contact for your organization, you'll simply have to focus on the commitment to develop relationship.

Notes

6
THE PRESS RELEASE

Every PR consultant must be able to create a press release that is written in compelling language so that people read them. Press releases should be written in a concise, accurate, and readable manner.

Before You Start

There is a process to follow when it comes to creating a press release that catches people's attention. If you don't follow the process it is still possible to get noticed, but also possible it won't or that you will leave out an important detail.

Before you start to write, ask yourself:

- Is your topic newsworthy? Some people think everything they do is newsworthy, or that everything outside of the usual routine is newsworthy. Make sure you look at your news from the perspective of the media and the public. If it's not newsworthy, it may be time to rethink what you are up to!
- Can you write the release in a way that it answers all the questions that it raises? That will help cut down on questions after you release it, and prevents turning off the journalist reading it who may not have time to call you.
- Will this release help to meet some part of the organization's strategic plan, and move it forward?
- Have you checked every piece of information in the release? All facts, data, dates, links, references must be accurate.

Once you can answer "yes" to all the questions above, you are ready to create the first draft of your press release, and not a moment before.

Release Information

First, if you are going to put out a press release, you should understand what a press release actually is. It is a vehicle for putting forth some newsworthy information. Topics can include a company expansion, an individual award, a new product release, a team championship or another topic in that vein. The scope is broad, but its aim is to be picked up as a story by the media. They can be included with a media package, but often they can stand alone.

It is a tool to get media coverage and hopefully have some journalists contact you to expand the release into a larger piece. But, despite that, you should always include all the information that is required to present a complete package. Don't leave something relevant out of the release in the hopes that a journalist will contact you to fill in the gaps.

Some press releases are more of a feature story that is put out by an organization, or individual, more than a news item. At times this distinction can be a fine one, but it is there. If you want to put out a feature story or tip, target some specific members of the media, or media outlets specifically, that are more likely to be interested in what you have to say rather than casting a very broad net and hoping for the best.

Contact Information

Okay, you've written a stunning press release and sent it to as many media outlets and contacts that you can think of. Then you sit back and wait and wait. Then you begin to wonder why no one has contacted you to follow up. You look at the release again, you've included all the pertinent information—everything except your contact information.

Don't find yourself in this situation. Include all your contact details. Highlight the one, or ones, that are most likely to reach you. If you have an email address that you only check one a week, you might as well leave it out, but if you do include it, make sure to check it often.

The Basics

Style

If you are just getting started in writing press releases, it is a good idea to go through an archive and see what the company has been releasing lately. These could be on their website or you may have to dig a little further but finding them is worth it to get a sense of tone and style they used. Then look at the results from those press releases, and whether they garnered the responses that were desired.

Catchy Headline

This is the first chance for you to differentiate yourself. Keep the headline short, valuable, and make it compelling so people read what is underneath it. While an editor who publishes your release will change your headline to match their publication or website, your job is to catch the editor's attention. If you are using e-mail (and you likely will) to submit a press release, your headline becomes your subject line.

Drafting

Start outlining your press release and working on the order that best expresses your news and ideas. Organize your writing to start with the most important elements first, so that if an editor must cut the size down, nothing essential is deleted. And, don't include anything that is not important, or you will put a dint in your credibility as you waste a reader's time.

Hard or Soft

Are most releases you are responsible for hard releases or soft? A hard release includes topics like new product releases, surveys, product releases, and staff appointments. A soft release, also called a feature release, can include updates of ongoing projects, trends, or human-interest stories.

Dates

Dates (there are two dates included: the first is the date the press release is issued, and the second is the date it is to be released.). Be careful. Don't send the release outside of your organization until you are ready for public release. Until then it remains an internal document only.

Contact

If you write the release, you should be the contact person most of the time. However, sometimes you need to direct inquiries to the spokesperson for a particular project, issue, or department. Include the name, e-mail, and contact number. If this release pertains to an emergency it is likely that an inquiry could come outside of regular business hours and you will need to include a cell phone number, too.

Design

Any public relations firm you use will have a design they follow for press releases. You can also set up a template, and if you see one you like, it doesn't hurt to adapt one. Developing a template, you can reuse is a great way to save yourself some time, but also creates a consistent look to your readers. Use consistent styles, and if your company has a style guide use it. Otherwise, use a media reference guide like The Associated Press Style book and Briefing on Media Law.

The Q & A List (Question and Answers)

If you can see that your press release will lead to some questions but don't answer them within the release itself, you can attach a sheet of answers to help people out. This is a great way to help members of your own executive that might have to field questions because you can give them a bit of background that is too wordy for the release.

Photos

Pictures are an excellent way to enhance your story. Each publication will have its own rules about submitting photos so that they can be reproduced properly. Always make sure that your pictures are of excellent, professional quality, and that they complement your story. Include a caption and the correct spelling for everyone who is in the picture, and you must be sure to cite sources and copyright information. If you have a good picture, your story will get more exposure than if it is a text-only story.

Eight Tips for a Successful Press Release

- Date, Location, and Topic at the top of the release.

- Keep it brief, no more than a page or two.

- One topic per paragraph.

- Use the inverted pyramid method. Put the most important information at the top and less important information as the press release continues.

- Use clear and short sentences in language that's easy to understand. Avoid jargon.

- Quotes are very good to give life to your press release.

- Keep a copy for yourself and send a copy to anyone that is quoted, or mentioned, in the release.

- At the end type –30– or –END– and center it at the bottom.

You don't make people secure by protecting them from things they don't want to encounter. The way to make people resilient is exposing them to things they are afraid of or makes them uncomfortable.

—*Mathew Knowles, M.B.A., Ph.D.*

Notes

7
PROVIDING INFORMATION TO THE MEDIA

When you are giving a quote to a member of the media, or providing some files, it's natural to wonder about that information. Is it safe? Is it going to be used accurately?

Security of Information and Files

When you are providing information to the media, sometimes you wish for it to remain private for whatever reason. Sometimes it's proprietary business information that you don't wish for a competitor to have, or perhaps it's personal information, or perhaps it's information that you are not supposed to have access to. But, despite all of that, you still wish to provide access to that material to the media, or perhaps a specific member of the media.

In that case, you will likely wonder about the security of the information you provide. Is it going to be hacked if you send it online, or is the member of the media going to leave it on the train on their commute home?

You can never be 100 per cent sure that the information you provide is going to be secure, that's the risk you take when you decide to provide it. The only way you can make sure that the information you have doesn't reach the wrong eyes or ears is to keep it to yourself. If you do not wish to follow that step, then there are few ways you can give yourself a modicum of peace of mind.

Note:
- Disposable email accounts allow you send an email, but then the account vanishes within a short period of allotted time. It is easy to find several of these online.
- Snapchat is a vehicle for providing short-lived information in a somewhat secure fashion.

There are some media outlets that promote the security they can provide for files that are entrusted to them. The Globe and Mail newspaper, in Toronto, Ontario, Canada, for instance runs ads that encourage sources to use their anonymous Secure Drop system, which operates through a Tor network, and have confidence when using it. They also use a PGP email system which allows messages, but not the sender's identity, to be encrypted. The New Yorker magazine uses this system as well.

Cyber security is a hot topic always, and if you're dealing with the media, it can be even more so. Take the steps to ensure that your computer and network is as secure as can be always. That will help make your information less open to being hacked.

Of course, there's always the old-fashioned way of having a paper copy of whatever information you wish to share and just letting the journalist look at, but not have a copy of, the document or documents. That way if there's only one copy, and you have it, you can rest assure that it won't be shared incorrectly or lost.

Attribution

When you are dealing with the media, and being interviewed, you should be clear on how the material, and the quotes, you are giving is going to be used. Of course, when you're being interviewed, the main one is 'on the record.' At times, you may want to keep information closely guarded, maybe 'off the record'. Some reporters say that there's no such thing as 'off the record' and whatever you say to them is fair game. That may be the case for them, but it's not the ethical way, and it's not fair.

Off the Record

This is one phrase that gets used a lot with the media, but it is also probably the most misunderstood phrase. People use it in the sense that 'You can't use what I'm going to tell you', but that's wrong.

What 'off the record' really means is: the information you are giving to a journalist can be used, but not with your name attached to it. It can be used as a stepping stone to gather more information. A journalist could take your off-the-record comment and follow up with another source in the manner of 'I have heard that' or 'A source told me that'.

It doesn't mean that the information you are giving to a member of the media is to go no farther than their own ears.

Confidential

Confidential is really what some people mean when they say, 'This is off the record.' If you give information to a journalist as confidential they are obliged, if they are ethical at all, to not use that information. It's a grown-up version of the kids' saying 'Okay, I'll tell you my secret, but you can't tell anyone.'

The journalist must keep your information in confidence, and if they want to explore what you've told them, they must find the same information elsewhere and totally keep you out of the resulting story or article. It's just as if you never told them at all.

Not-for-Attribution

This is more of the unnamed source type of media relationship. You are giving information to a member of the media, and give them consent to use it, but you don't give consent for your name to be attached to it. In this case, your identity must be known by the media outlet, at the very least by the reporter and the editor.

Different Types of Media

The days of the reporter with the press pass stuck into the hat band of a fedora are long, long gone. Citizen journalism is a powerful force. Everyone can quickly and easily capture photos, videos, and audio recordings and have that information online within minutes. These citizen journalists are the watchdogs of the world. Social media has evened the playing field when it comes to breaking a story or getting a message to the public.

Social media journalism is now fully entrenched in the news media landscape. Think of the stories you have seen or read that cite online posts or comments or blogs as sources. Not only that, there are plenty of sites that bill themselves as crowd-sourced news sites, think of ones like Digital Journal, Newsvine, Wikinews, GlobalVoices, and CNN iReport. Other sites such as Street Reporter offer training for citizen journalists.

Often, mainstream media solicits input form citizen journalists, increasing their sources and coverage areas.

However, that's not to say that the tradition media outlets of newspapers, radio, and TV have lost their prominence. Calling someone and saying you're from The New York Times still carries some weight with it.

But more than reputation, another major factor to consider is resources, when you can have a widespread team of people working on a story, it can produce a work with depth.

So never forget, when you're dealing with someone, especially in an official capacity, that your words can be soon made public, even if it's not your intention. That's not to say you should be wary or paranoid, but as the old saying goes: "Don't do (or in this case say) something in public that you wouldn't want your mother to see you doing."

Keeping Copies of Interviews

"I was taken out of context."

Sound familiar? How many times have you heard someone make that claim in the media when something they've said has become a problem for them?

It's a convenient way to attempt to deflect criticism by blaming it on the media and saying that's not exactly what the speaker meant. Don't let this happen to you. If you're being interviewed, you have every right to record it for yourself as well. That protects you and holds the journalist accountable too.

In media scrums, press conferences, or other interviews it isn't unusual to see PR representatives and/or communications officer recording the Q&A when their client is speaking. It's mostly a case of 'better safe than sorry.'

Of course, it's always easier to keep a copy of your remarks if you are conducting an email interview or issuing a prepared statement, but it's easy to record as well. There's no reason to be the one claiming to be 'taken out of context.'

It's not "I" it's "we" that's what makes a team.

—Mathew Knowles, M.B.A., Ph.D.

Notes

DEVELOPING MEDIA RELATIONSHIPS

If you deal with someone on a regular, or somewhat regular, you are going to develop a relationship with them, whether it's totally professional, personal, or somewhere in between.

Professional vs. Personal

If you deal with the media long enough, you will develop relationships with some journalists, it's human nature. These professional relationships are a two-way street, treat the journalist with respect and it's bound to flow both ways.

It's best to keep these working relationships as professional, sometimes tough questions must be asked, and answered, and it's a bit easier if you're not dealing with a friend.

Media Contact Lists

This is actually more of a concern for the professional communications officer or spokesperson, but if you're the media person for a minor hockey team or charitable event, it's a good idea to have a list of media contacts.

Rather than just using a shotgun approach and blasting your message out to everyone you can think of, it's a good idea to curate your list so it hits the members of the media most likely to be interested in your message and pass it along. There's no point in sending your minor hockey scores to a national TV journalist but the sports editor for the local radio station makes perfect sense.

Providing Tips/Story Ideas to Media

The media, professional and citizen-led, is always hungry for more information, more news, more stories. A lot of story leads come from ideas that are submitted by the public at large. But how do you get those ideas to the media? It's easy, media outlets need to produce stories and any help they can get, they will take. To that end, they have multiple contact details on their websites, business cards, and so on.

If you can couch your story tip in a way that highlights its originality or show that it will be a 'scoop', then it has a much better chance at being acted upon by a member of media. Show why the journalist should care about this tip.

How do you choose who to send your story tip to? As mentioned above, think about the tip itself, it's not much good sending a business news tip to a citizen journalist who specializes in writing about religious matters.

Who to Choose

This is where developing a relationship with the media comes in handy. You know the media person, or persons, who are most likely to be interested in your idea. Also, if you respect someone and their work, you are more likely to send a tip their way.

As a journalist, it also works the same way, if you treat a source professionally, and with courtesy, they are more likely to give you a scoop or some inside information they may withhold from others. That can be tricky ground though, if you're bestowed with that trust don't abuse it.

People buy you first and then your product.

—Mathew Knowles, M.B.A., Ph.D.

Notes

PR AND THE CRISIS

Sometimes things go wrong. When a strike, a recall, a weather bomb, or something unexpected comes along, it's up to the PR consultant to manage the communications.

Business Continuity and Recovery

Crisis communications have a different intensity than much of our other work, but the essence is the same in that you must communicate effectively, consistently, and in a timely manner.

Setting Priorities

When you have determined what urgent and non-urgent aspects of the business need to be restored to maintain the integrity of the business and meet stakeholder expectations, you will know what needs to be done first. Often, we will review each major function of the business to determine what activities are essential, and how much time we can tolerate for any function to be unavailable.

For example, a hospital may be unable to tolerate any time at all for an emergency department to be closed. The tolerance for that part of the business to be unavailable is zero.

Within the same hospital, though, they may be able to tolerate the kitchen being unavailable for up to three hours and still meet the needs of their patients.

However, if the kitchen is destroyed, there could be an expectation that food could be secured from another location (i.e. another hospital across town) within the three-hour window. Another example would be that a fast-food restaurant could close for a 24-hour period with virtually no effect on customers, who could go somewhere else. (Shareholders might find it unsatisfactory, however.

If the local state building becomes inaccessible, the fact that renewals for drivers' licenses cannot be processed is not as big of a problem as the inability to issue checks for welfare or social services benefits.

Essential Crisis Plan Elements

Every organization will have different answers to the question, "what is critical for us?" but what's important is to have the conversation and decide what is important together.

> **I don't have a problem if you aim high and miss, but I am going to have a real issue if you aim low and hit.**
>
> —*Mathew Knowles, M.B.A., Ph.D.*

Notes

SOCIAL MEDIA AND PUBLIC RELATIONS

Successful people think outside of the box rather than inside the box. We've been conditioned as early as childhood and told things we could never accomplish. I call that "box end thinking."

Where It Is

Social media is a firmly established element of the media, and it's going to continue to evolve and wrap its way throughout our lives in intangible ways. Every press release, public appearance, annual report, as well as aspects of information that used to be kept protected, are now found within social media.

Social media is everywhere. If you're going to embrace your role within public relations, you need to embrace social media, too.

Monitoring Tips and Tricks

There are several ways that you can keep an eye on your environment to know what kind of things are being said about your company, and you as an individual. In the old days, it was common practice for a staffer to scour newspaper headlines and magazines, cut the noteworthy articles out, paste them in a collection, and circulate them in a file folder for everyone to read.

It is much easier to let other members of the company know what's being said in the media, because you can set up Google Alerts to tell you every time your company name or certain keywords are mentioned, search social networking sites, and even coordinate aggregate collections. Whichever methods you use, make sure that you are consistent about looking, and that you have a process set up for responding.

Monitoring processes are especially effective when customers complain. For example, if a customer does not like something about a product you sell and they announce their dissatisfaction on Twitter, your reputation is somewhat restored when you quickly reply and see to their needs. Ignoring their messages, however, means that the complainer can add more and more messages and your lack of response annoys them more and more.

Remember: failure to plan is planning to fail.

—Mathew Knowles, M.B.A., Ph.D.
The DNA of Achievers: 10 Traits of Highly Successful Professionals

Notes

SPEAKING UNDER PRESSURE?

Speaking Under Pressure is about building skills for dealing with unsympathetic audiences. It addresses some of your worst fears about being on the spot. This exercise presents techniques to organize ideas in pressure situations or when no advance preparation time is available.

The core of this exercise is developing thinking strategies which guide our ability to analyze, organize, and present ideas. At the end of the exercise, you will be able to quickly organize and structure a presentation, deliver a convincing message without speaker's notes, and provide sound and convincing answers to the most difficult questions.

How do you prepare for most of your speaking engagements? We're going to use a technique that is used throughout the world, and yet remains unknown to most people. This technique has been adapted by large speaker training organizations such as Toastmasters International. To plan each speaking opportunity, whether it is two minutes or an hour, we use an opening, body, and closing. We stress that you prepare as much as possible, yet still allow for flexibility. Then you practice, practice, and practice.

There is an old saying: "Be careful what you think, for these become your words. Be careful of your words, for they become your actions. Be careful of your actions, for they become your habits. Be careful of your habits, for they become your character. Be careful of your character, for your character becomes your destiny."

All we really need to get from this is that clear thinking will usually result in clear speaking, and generally we become clearer at what we want to say as we think and plan our approach.

So that our clear thinking is evident to others, it's important that we are perceived as organized and prepared. That means having an opening, a body, and a closing, when we are presenting or responding to a question. For people who want to get ahead in life (which most of us do!), developing the ability to speak with clarity is one of the greatest talents we can cultivate.

One way to get clarity is to write our thoughts down on paper or to work them out on a computer. A second way is to practice speaking with clarity. Perhaps the best technique is to combine these two: write our thoughts down and practice saying them out loud.

Planning

If required to speak under trying circumstances, you need to plan to get good at this.

What Can You Do for Better Planning?
Be informed.

You can't do much planning if you don't know much about a topic. Learn all you can about the topics you might be expected to give an opinion on. Read your local newspaper and credible online resources. Read albums (but be careful about reading just one album). Read magazines like Time and Maclean's that have some real content about the issues of the day. Talk to your manager, your colleagues, and your staff so you know their opinion or any expertise they bring to the table.

Don't Make Up Your Mind Too Early

Keeping an open mind as you gather information is not easy, yet decisions we make in haste are ones that we often regret later. Try to keep analyzing the information as you get it. Is it accurate? Do you understand it? What can you do to be more informed?

Ask Questions

Don't assume that you have heard everything there is to hear, or that you understand a concept entirely the first time you hear it. Thoughtful people and critical thinkers will give themselves time to pause and reflect before commenting either positively or negatively on an idea. Asking questions and developing your listening skills to get all you can from the answers are two important communication skills to practice and develop.

Be Aware of Your Own Biases

We all have some, so they are nothing to be ashamed of. However, if we know what our biases are, we can keep them from influencing our decisions too strongly.

Weigh Opinions Against the Facts

Try not to be influenced by others' opinions or emotions until you have considered all the facts. This is another way our biases can trip us up: you like a person so you give their opinion more weight than you should, or more weight than the facts (which may contradict that opinion). Or, conversely, you don't like a person, so you disregard their opinion even when it is supported by facts.

Keep the Information You Gather Organized

Write down all the information you gather, or at least make notes about what you still want more information on. Identify the criteria you will use for evaluating the information. List the pros and cons, the costs and benefits, or use force field analysis (which we will discuss later).

Watch for Traps

Be aware of these ways your transfer of ideas can be confused, if you aren't prepared:

- Derailment: Somebody asks you a question and you lose your train of thought or head down another path, never to return to the path you originally were on.

- Rocky Mountain Road: Your presentation has no real theme or plan. You just stumble from point to point. Neither you nor your audience is sure whether you will arrive at the end of your presentation.

- Roller Coaster: You make a good strong point, followed by a more obscure point, back to a strong point again, rather than starting with your best shot and working down to the details, or starting with the details and working up to your main point.

- Whirlpool: You say the same things repeatedly, without getting anywhere or presenting new information.

Overcoming Nervousness

Slight nervousness is normal for anyone, especially the first few times you make a presentation or speak in public. These jitters can actually help you and give you an edge when you take that nervous energy and deliberately use it as fuel for your presentation.

Nervousness has a way of spiraling, where you may notice suddenly that your heart is pounding, your knees are shaking, or your voice is trembling. Here are some helpful tips to get control back.

The secret you want to learn is not necessarily the confidence that comes from experience, although that helps, but a change in attitude. When you learn to shift your focus from yourself to the audience, you start to release the hold that fear has on you.

One of things that you will notice is that when you are well prepared for your presentation, you will feel less nervous about it. While confidence can be built from repeated practice, a change in attitude also helps enormously. This requires that you shift your thinking from being all about you, to focusing on your audience. *What are their needs? What is their agenda?*

Nervousness can be attributed to many sources. These two are particularly important:

- One is the constant stream of internal negative comments that nags speakers when they begin to think about the presentation. ("I wonder how I'll come across this time? Last time I made a presentation, I was sure everyone was laughing at me when I had so much trouble with the equipment.")
- The other source of tension comes from hyper-responsibility.

The presenter feels that he or she alone is responsible for the reactions and well-being of everyone in the room.

Think about it this way: you believe in what you're saying. You're prepared. In fact, for this presentation, you're the only person who is so well prepared. Your audience needs to know what you have to say.

Change the words you say to yourself from negative messages to more positive ones. List your concerns on a sheet of paper before the presentation. Then, for every negative message, substitute a positive one. For instance, if your negative message is, "I'm a nervous wreck," write, "I can channel this nervous energy into the presentation and give a more enthusiastic performance." This effort may take some repetitions, but if you give it a chance and believe in it, eventually it works.

Any tendency you have toward taking responsibility for everyone in the room can also be fought. Come to terms with the fact that everyone in the room will not necessarily accept your ideas. It's not your job to please everyone. Your job is to get your message across in clearly understandable terms to the people who must have the information. Concentrate on the decision maker and on those who respond positively to you. Ignore the others so that you can complete your presentation without their negative energy interfering.

It is hard to counteract nervousness if you do not feel in control of the situation, so take time before the presentation begins to put yourself in control.

- Allow plenty of time to check out the room and equipment.
- Start on time. Unless the decision maker in your audience is delayed, don't wait for stragglers. Delaying will make you and your audience fidgety.
- Greet people as they come in. Chat casually with people you know until it's time to start.
- Eliminate any physical barriers that stand between the audience and you. If you're behind a table or lectern, move away from it. Don't cling to the podium or your projector. It makes you look nervous, and it really is a physical barrier between you and your audience. Removing barriers opens the way to meaningful conversation.

Sequencing Ideas

By putting your ideas into order, it will be easier for you to remember and easier for your listener to grasp your ideas.

- Study: Break your ideas into simple, basic components.
- Separate: Present each component separately.
- Move Forward: By building momentum successively with each component, you gain and keep your listener's interest.

This is another way of being prepared and controlling your jitters.

Ensuring Your Listener Hears You

Use Nonverbal Communication

You're confident. You've rehearsed. You've got a powerful, logical argument. You're ready to take on the task of presenting your points in a way that does not distract from your argument. In management presentations, the drama should be in the content, not in the person. Once you're aware of the way people react to you, you can further refine the way you present yourself.

Leave the Appropriate Distance between You and the Audience

Although a public speaker may be 12 to 15 feet from the first row of listeners without being viewed as aloof and impersonal, a management presenter (who generally deals with far fewer people) should be no more than four to five feet away. If you're any farther away, the listeners may regard you as either stuffy or fearful. If you get any closer, people will become uncomfortable.

When you're speaking to a group with whom you have had little or no personal or professional relationship, start speaking from a position farther away and move in slightly as the presentation progresses and as you establish rapport. But don't get too close. A tall presenter, for example, who approaches within inches of his listeners and leans forward, is expressing dominance more than friendliness. To judge whether you tend to invade others' personal space, recall whether people ever inched away from you when you were engaged in informal conversations.

Physical distance rules vary from one culture to another. Some people often want to be within inches of each other when they speak, whereas others expect even more distance than you might be used to. Make sure that you know your audience.

Stand Erect

Good posture gives the impression of authority. You can correct poor posture by standing against a wall and pressing your spine flat against it. Feel what it is like to be standing straight and make the most of it.

While you're making your presentation, make a conscious effort not to fold your arms. Folded arms seem to encourage slouching, and it certainly sends a message of defending or protecting yourself. There is a difference between good posture and stiffness, however. If you march briskly to the front of the room and do not move for the rest of the presentation, you signal rigidity more than authority.

Consider Your Appearance

Psychologists have found that attractive people are more persuasive than unattractive people. Anyone can cultivate attractiveness through good grooming and clean, neat, professional dress. A presentation is not the place to make a statement with your clothes—flashy clothes divert attention from your argument.

The standard business dress is suits or jackets and a tie for men although tie decorum has changed. I personally never wear a tie! But I'm comfortable with that. Conservative suits or coordinated outfits are standard business dress for women. Although standards in non-traditional organizations may be more lenient, in general it is safer to stay on the side of conservatism. Anything too far from the norm will cause the audience to fix on the distracting feature rather than your argument. You want to convey competence in the subject matter, and what you wear can support you or undermine you.

Move About and Use Gestures

A presenter who stays glued to the overhead projector, the lectern, or any other one position is quite possibly terrified, and everyone soon knows it. To give the impression of self-confidence, move about the room and use your hands. Behaving like a confident presenter will help you to become more confident.

Take advantage of your natural gestures but avoid using one over and over. Some presenters, when told that they need to add movement, adopt one gesture (raising an arm, for example) and use it repeatedly.

At worst, such programmed gestures send the audience into a hypnotic state; at best, they're distracting. Tailor your gestures to reinforce your point. For instance, by bringing your hands together, you can assure your audience that your proposal "brings it all together." Similarly, you can refer to the ramifications of a problem by tracing ever-widening circles in the air.

Because most management presentations involve visual aids, you can add movement by simply pointing out the most important features on the visual. Moving around the room is helpful if it does not deteriorate into the measured pacing of a caged tiger. By pausing completely, you will emphasize the importance of what you are saying.

Control Your Facial Expressions and Mannerisms

Although we all know people who say, "If you cut off my hands, I wouldn't be able to talk," very few people overdo gestures.

Facial expressions, on the other hand, are difficult to control and often give an embarrassingly accurate clue as to how you really feel. Beyond checking yourself on videotape, the best way to control facial expressions is to make sure you're comfortable with your material and prepared to respond honestly and openly to any questions.

Try to maintain an accessible, open presence. Remember that a smile breaks down barriers. When you smile at someone, they generally smile back. Also, as you talk, show interest in what you're saying. If you're not interested, how can your audience be?

Maintain Eye Contact

You will lose support faster by staring at your notes, looking only at the visual, or focusing on a spot high on the back wall than by any mistakes you may make in the content of your presentation. Similarly, if you direct yourself exclusively to the key decision maker in your audience, he or she will feel more uneasy than flattered, and others in the room will feel unimportant.

Try, at some point in the presentation, to look at each participant with the goal of giving each, in turn, the brief message, "I can see that you grasp what I'm saying." Then, for your own comfort, focus on people who respond with a nod or smile rather than on people who seem bored or hostile.

The Value of a Pause

If you are speaking within a negative or outright hostile situation, it is easy to become defensive and even angry. Instead of quickly answering every question (which increases the pressure and makes it difficult to maintain your composure), explore the value of a pause. A pause can give you a mini-break to collect your thoughts and deliver them well. It can also stop you from getting caught in an angry or emotional outburst.

Use pauses to your advantage. If someone asks a question and you need to collect your thoughts, you can take a moment to glance at your notes if you are using some, take a deep breath (not noticeable to anyone else), and then answer.

Failure is an opportunity to grow not a reason to quit. Ego is the anesthesia that deadens the pain of stupidity.
—*Mathew Knowles, M.B.A., Ph.D.*

Notes

FOCUSING YOUR MESSAGE

By taking aim and finding a key theme, you will be able to focus your message specifically to your individual listener.

What is a Key Theme?

By putting yourself in your listeners' shoes, you can often find out what approach would make this topic understandable and interesting to them. When you make it as straightforward and simple as possible, you'll have a theme that holds their attention.

Why Use a Key Theme?

- A key theme helps you plan.
- It also helps keep you on track.
- It leads your listener to your conclusion or recommendations.
- It holds your listener's attention and helps prevent boredom.
- Key themes help convey a memorable message. They also help your listener remember your message.

How Do I Find a Key Theme?

You may find your key theme by using experience from the past in dealing with this listener or common sense.

When you are defining your key theme, you can take a direct approach and ask a member of your future audience for their help. Discussing your topic with someone else can help you clearly articulate what you need to say.

Empathy is critical as you consider the needs of your audience. Your approach will be different (and your theme will be different) when you speak to teenagers about drinking and driving than it would be if you were speaking to Mothers Against Drunk Driving (MADD).

Key Sentences

After you have discovered and written down your key theme, take your virtual scissors and cut it down to key words: a 3 to 7-word sentence that will become your introduction (beginning) and conclusion (ending). This key sentence must be strong and impressionable.

Why Use a Key Sentence?

- It is a short, direct statement that focuses you onto your key theme.
- It leaves your listener with a simple idea that keeps your message alive.
- It sums up your message with minimal distortion.

How Do I Write a Key Sentence?

- Talking straight and simply
- Using short, direct, familiar, concrete, single, short, words
- Creating pictures to hold the audience's attention
- Keeping adjectives and adverbs to a minimum
- Using active tense, not passive
- Keeping it simple and avoiding clutter

Remember: Stop, Think, Plan, React

- Scan the situation
- Decide on your objective
- Create your plan
- Keep your eye on the objective

Structuring Ideas

Three Key Points

We have already been working on a three-part plan: opening, body, and closing for every presentation or response we make. However, now we are going to zero in on the body of your plan, to make your message as persuasive as possible.

Remember, the essence of Speaking Under Pressure is quick and structured thinking which allows you to persuade your listener. What you want is a memorable message conveyed quickly and clearly. You have defined your strategy and done some preparation work. You are now ready to create planned approaches and to practice some new skills.

Why Three Key Points?

We recommend that you outline three key points for the body of your presentation. Your introduction (beginning) and conclusion (ending) will be short additions to your key points. Let's talk about why we recommend three key parts.

Aim

To send a memorable message, you must aim your presentation in a logical and organized manner. You want to leave no doubt in your listener's mind what you are trying to say. He/she must be able to catch the essence of your presentation. So, let's stick to facts, ideas, and points of view that are best suited to your particular listener.

You want your listeners to catch the softball aimed at them. They should not have to duck out of the way of a muddy message. Having only three points will help you create a clear target for your presentation.

Make sure you have already found out what your audience wants to hear and figure out how you can give them at least some of what they want. Try to speak in clear, easy to understand words and sentences. We don't trust people we don't understand.

Concentrate

You must have a plan for you to concentrate on clear thinking. The stronger your sense of organization, the less likely you will become confused or hampered by emotions and personal opinions.

By using your pre-programmed plan, keeping it simple and direct, you make your point clearly. If your thoughts have been well organized, they will be clear and easy to present. This means that you can give your full attention to getting your message across and looking and sounding confident and sincere as you watch your audience.

Adapt

You must have a good grasp of the purpose of your presentation so that you are free to scan the situation repeatedly; to read and to react to your listener's needs and wishes. By having a plan, you will be free to adjust to and explain ideas which are aimed at your individual listener's needs.

Adapt when necessary. Watch for agreement: eye contact, a smile, a nod of the head. Watch for confusion: a wrinkled brow, a quizzical expression. Watch for disagreement: a scowl, folded arms, inattention. Then you can react as required. Get feedback. Add examples. Allow questions.

Depth

We learned that planning helps to cure jitters and that planning is simple. Planning involves the orderly sequence of ideas (study, separate, move forward). In order to create some depth to the study, there must be enough components or parts.

Two points are too few, yet five or six might be too many for people to consider at one time. Three or four points work best because they are simple yet offer opportunity for analysis.

Move Forward

We noted that it is important to have a dynamic presentation, one that moves along. Three points offer enough components to create a sense of motion; perhaps even a sense of anticipation.

Ease

Three points are easy to remember; therefore, easy to present and convey.

Organization Methods

Using Time, Place, and Aspect

Experienced presenters and speakers often use a single piece of paper, file cards or sticky notes when they collect information, since they can be easily arranged and rearranged. By arranging them in piles, you can create an organizational plan and add or delete information without the need to redo the entire presentation. There are also software programs that enable this kind of simple reorganizing.

Here are the steps to organizing your information.

1. Write only one point on each card or sticky note or single piece of paper.

2. Arrange the cards into piles, putting all closely related points together. For example, all evidence related to economic development goes in one pile, all evidence related to profiling the community goes in another pile, and so on.

3. Arrange the piles in one of the following basic ways:

   - **Time:** Organize information from past to present to future. The time plan is easy to picture (clock, day/night, etc.) and to create. Use of past, present, future can often help make sense out of any jumble of facts, especially when you have little time to prepare.

   - **Place:** Everyone can visualize a map or globe as you travel with your listener from place to place. The place plan lends itself to topics which are geographically separated. Remember to leave the most important place for last for maximum impact. You may want to create forward motion by arranging items in geographical direction.

   - **Aspect, Factor, or Focus:** Examining the topic from different perspectives. Visualize an equidistant triangle. You examine the key theme from three different points. You will find this plan especially helpful in serious situations when you want to create the impression of being fair-minded.

   - **Problem-analysis-solution:** Description of the problem, why it exists, and what to do about it.

   - **Order of Importance:** From least important to most important, or from most important to least important.

   - **The choice of sequence:** This will depend largely on the logic of the subject matter and the needs of your audience.

4. Go through each pile and arrange the cards or sticky notes in an understandable sequence within your basic plan. Which points need to precede others to present a clear picture?

5. Write out your organization plan to create an outline. Use it as your road map while you write your message.

Two Additional Plans

The methods we just discussed are the most common ways of organizing material before you present it. However, there are many other options. Here are two examples.

Zoom Lens

You may start with a specific example and then move to a more general perspective, such as from one car manufacturer to the whole industry. (This is called the divergent approach.) The reverse can also work: moving from a general perspective to a specific example. (This is called the convergent approach.)

Pendulum Plan

This examines the issues in terms of extremes, such as no businesses open on Sunday to every business open on Sunday, and then settles on a mid-point where some businesses are open on Sunday. This can be difficult to do successfully yet it can also be a very effective way of demonstrating your ability to compromise or to seek a middle ground.

The Meaning Behind Our Message

While our words deliver a significant message, our non-verbal signals also provide their own message. You know that you are in sync when the two are working together!

In significant (though often misinterpreted) research, Albert Mehrabian found that when it came to discussing emotions, only 7% of the speaker's message was communicated by words, and that tone of voice was responsible for about 38% of the meaning and body language about 55%. This means that the words themselves played only a very small part in conveying meaning. In other conversations (not the ones about emotions), we know that tone of voice and body language have a large impact on what we are saying.

The face and the eyes are the most expressive means of body communication. Additional positive or negative messages are sent by your gestures, posture, and the space between you and the other person. Body language must be in tune with your words and tone or you send a mixed and often confusing message. Positive body language is important to supporting your words and ensuring complete understanding.

Remember, your attitude is projected through your voice as well as your body language. Make sure your body language always says, "I know what I'm doing and saying," or, "I'm here to help as best I can." The speed or rhythm of your speech is important as well. Clear communication includes appropriate pauses and inflections to support your words.

Qualities of a Good Voice

- Alert: Awake and interested
- Pleasant: A smile in your voice (when appropriate)
- Natural: Straightforward language, without jargon
- Enthusiastic: Glad to speak
- Distinct: Easy to understand with moderate volume and rate
- Expressive: Well-modulated, varied tone

Beginnings and Endings

Some general points about beginnings and endings:

- You really do only get one chance to make a first impression, so make it good and make it count. If you lose their attention at the beginning, it's hard to get it back. Make things easier on yourself with a good hook.
- The beginning and ending must be coherent with the content of your message; they must add to the unity of the overall presentation.
- The beginning and ending should be a brief indication of what is to come and a summary of what has been. You don't have to build in a surprise.
- The duties of the beginning and ending are to highlight your key theme, send out a mental picture of where you are going, and to make the plan move forward.

There are three purposes to a good beginning:

- Orient your listener to your key theme. State it directly and indicate exactly what it is you are going to talk about.
- Provide them with a sense of direction by summarizing your outline in the beginning.
- Hint to your listener what your conclusion will be.

An Ending Should:

- Summarize what you have just said.
- Finish by restating your key theme. You want to reinforce your message and leave your key theme as a residual element that listeners will continue to think about.

- Empower your audience

When Writing an Ending, You Should:

- Stop: Pause. Take a moment to reflect on your message.

- Think: Study, compartmentalize, and analyze to ensure you are seeing things from the audience's point of view.

- Plan: Review your outline and then prepare an ending that wraps up your message. Consider whether you also need to tell them what their next steps are.

- React: Respond to your listener, audience, or customer to give them what's needed.

Expanding a Basic Plan

So far, we've concentrated most of our efforts on very short, two-minute responses, because these are the opportunities to speak that most often come our way and that we want to use to our advantage. Generally, longer presentations are not spontaneous. You've been forewarned of longer presentations, so you have time to prepare.

However, you may want to take what we've discussed and use those ideas to make a longer presentation. This session will give you some ideas on how to fatten up your basic plan by filling in the subsections and reinforcing your argument. In this process, you can include evidence that supports your key theme. The results of your audience analysis should allow you to pick examples and illustrations at the listener's knowledge level which will clarify your points. The listener's attitudes will also influence what evidence you use to prove your points.

Some techniques that can help you build on your basic plan are listed below.

Symbols

Use fat words that paint pictures, rather than thin words that leave no impression on our minds. Find the most striking circumstances involved with whatever you are describing. A well-chosen example can be so powerful that it becomes the focus for the point being illustrated.

Opposites

Compare and contrast. Getting a solid idea of similarities and differences can make decision making easier. For example, if you are debating what kind of coffee to have in the office, you can compare fair trade with open market coffee by assessing their similarities. If you wish to provide contrast, you must assess the differences between two things.

Statistics

Statistics can be rounded off or made specific. When rounded off, they are easier for the audience to remember. When they are more specific, the audience gives the stats more credibility but may have difficulty remembering the figures. What method will best work for your audience, give you credibility, and be remembered?

Tips and Tricks

Be sure that any extra content strengthens your conclusion or recommendations.

You can vary the type of plan you use to create interest and maintain your listener's attention. If your boss has heard your short presentation once or twice and has invited a few guests in to hear your full idea, remember that you must keep him engaged as well. This can be especially important when they are considering several presentations and will select what projects will get priority, for example.

You can vary the number of subsections to create movement. Review but don't restate too often or you run the risk of becoming boring. Sometimes we get into a rhythm where we put a new slide up, say five sentences, and move onto the next slide. Mix it up and be memorable. Your presentation needs to focus on your message, not the number of slides you can pack together.

People love stories, and a story helps us to remember the point if it is memorable and connected to your presentation. Resist the temptation to use other people's stories and look at your own. See if you can adapt it to fit your point and add some variety and/or meaning to your presentation.

Notes

PUBLIC RELATIONS AND MEDIA WORK BOOK

OVERVIEW

Why did you buy this book? Use this opportunity to consider how this book fits into your personal learning journey.

_____
_____
_____
_____
_____
_____
_____
_____
_____

Identify and briefly describe several businesses that you find interesting. Include a couple of sentences about how each business approaches their public relations, and whether they are positive, negative, successful, or not with their efforts.

_____
_____
_____
_____
_____
_____
_____
_____

Notes

1
PUBLIC RELATIONS

What public relations campaigns have you observed that have a positive influence on public relations as a field of study?

Do you have stories of public relations blunders that you have learn from?

Notes

2
BUILDING YOUR PR PLAN

We know that using tactics will get us a certain distance, but that PR programs become more successful with higher results and better market penetration when they are built on strategy. Define your strategy and tactics.

_____
_____
_____
_____
_____
_____
_____
_____
_____
_____

Create a draft document that outlines your PR strategy and tactical plan for an upcoming project.

_____
_____
_____

Record ideas to improve your plan.

_____
_____
_____

Notes

3
STRUCTURING MESSAGES

What kind of relationship do you/your company have with members of the media today?
_____
_____
_____
_____
_____

Do you have a media strategy?
_____
_____
_____
_____
_____

When was the last time you read or saw something about your company in the news? Was it good news, or not? Was it well written?
_____
_____
_____
_____
_____
_____

Write a two-paragraph bio of yourself that can be included in a media package.

What additional aspects would you add to the MEDIA model?

Notes

ESTABLISHING MEDIA GUIDELINES AND MANAGING THE MEDIA

Develop a list of media guidelines for you or your company.

_____
_____
_____
_____
_____
_____
_____
_____
_____
_____
_____
_____
_____

Brainstorm some sources for information that a media spokesperson can make use of that a member of the media might not have access to.

_____
_____
_____
_____

Notes

5
BEING INTERVIEWED

Create a sound bite that is pertinent to you personally, or to a product or service that your company offers.

Notes

THE PRESS RELEASE

How could you handle a situation when some of the answers are "no" and your organization wants you to proceed with a release?

Complete the press release form below for an upcoming product, staff appointment, or some other event.

Press Release Form

The Basics

Issue Date: _____

Release Date: _____

Catchy Headline: _____

Contact Person Information

Name: _____

Contact number: _____

E-mail address: _____

The Body

Write your text. Use compelling, concise language, and be sure to cover the 5 W's (who, what, why, where, when) and how as appropriate. Limit yourself to two pages maximum. Start with the most important information at the top of your document, with supporting details to follow. That way if some information needs to be edited out to fit into available space, all your important details are included.

_____
_____
_____
_____
_____
_____
_____
_____
_____
_____
_____
_____
_____
_____
_____
_____
_____

Final Points

Q & A required? .... Yes/No

Photo attached? .... Yes/No

Approvals received? .... Yes/No

Notes

PROVIDING INFORMATION TO THE MEDIA

Search for various media outlets online and see what types of security promises or guarantees they make to their sources.

Notes

DEVELOPING MEDIA RELATIONSHIPS

Think about any interactions you have had with members of the media. Did you initiate it? Was it positive or negative? Would you do something differently?

_____
_____
_____
_____
_____
_____
_____
_____
_____
_____
_____
_____

Develop a contact list of journalists, at the local, regional, or national level, or perhaps all three levels if you want. Then consider what type of stories should be sent to their journalists.

_____
_____
_____
_____
_____
_____

Notes

PR AND THE CRISIS

Use the space below to write a press release for a project you are working on.

_____
_____
_____
_____
_____
_____
_____
_____
_____
_____
_____

Create a Q & A list for the press release you just wrote.

_____
_____
_____
_____
_____
_____
_____
_____
_____
_____
_____

Notes

SOCIAL MEDIA AND PUBLIC RELATIONS

Where do your company's messages appear in media, including social media?
_____
_____
_____
_____
_____
_____
_____
_____
_____

What kind of monitoring do you currently do?
_____
_____
_____
_____
_____
_____
_____
_____
_____
_____

Are you using Google Alerts or a similar system effectively?

Do you have a communications company helping you to manage your public image?

What do you need to change?

Personal Action Plan

Now that you have completed the book and work book Public Relations and Media, how will you use the things you have learned? Creating a personal action plan can help you stay on track and on target. When you take responsibility for yourself and your results, you get things done!

I am already doing these things well:
___
___
___
___
___
___

I want to improve these areas:
___
___
___
___
___
___

I have these resources to help me:
___
___
___
___
___
___

As a result of what I have learned, I am going to...
___
___
___
___
___
___

My target date is...

I will know I have succeeded when...

I will follow up with myself on...

Notes

ABOUT THE AUTHOR

Dr. Mathew Knowles has an MBA in Business and Strategic Planning and a doctorate in Business Administration for Strategic Leadership and Organizational Culture. Bestowed the honor of Doctor of Humane Letters from his alma mater, Fisk, in 2008; he also taught there for two years. He is the founder, President, and CEO of Music World Entertainment, Inc. With record sales exceeding 300 million worldwide, he established several recording imprints and was crowned by Billboard magazine as one of the Top Imprint Labels of the decade (2000-2009). Under Knowles' guidance, Destiny's Child was named on Billboard Magazine's Top 10 Artists of the Decade (2000-2009).

For the past eight years, he has instructed in "Introduction to the Recording Industry, Artist Management" for undergraduates, and "Media Entrepreneurship" on a graduate level at Texas Southern University, as a visiting professor in their School of Communication in the Entertainment, Recording, Management (ERM) degree program.

For more information go to **Mathewknowles.com**

www.ingramcontent.com/pod-product-compliance
Lightning Source LLC
Chambersburg PA
CBHW081115080526
44587CB00021B/3603